HAPPY BIRTHDAY

NOW YOU ARE

THREE

D1361705

3

3

First edition for the United States and Canada published in 1995
by Barron's Educational Series, Inc.

© Copyright 1994 Quartz Editorial Services, 112 Station Road,
Edgware HA8 7AQ United Kingdom.

All inquiries should be addressed to:
Barron's Educational Series, Inc.
250 Wireless Boulevard
Hauppauge, NY 11788

International Standard Book No. 0-8120-9417-4

Library of Congress Catalog Card No. 95-11456

Library of Congress Cataloging-in-Publication Data
Happy birthday, now you are three / illustrations by Clare Heronneau.—
    1st ed.
        p.   cm.
    ISBN 0-8120-9417-4
    1. Three (The number)—Juvenile literature.   2. Number concept—
    Juvenile literature.   [1. Three. (The number)   2. Number concept.]
    I. Heronneau, Clare, ill.
    QA141.15.H364   1995
    513.2' 11–dc20   95-11456
                                                          CIP
                                                          AC

Printed in Hong Kong
5678 9955 987654321

HAPPY BIRTHDAY

NOW YOU ARE

THREE

ILLUSTRATIONS BY
CLARE HERONNEAU

BARRON'S

THREE CANDLES ON YOUR CAKE!

HOW MANY WHEELS DOES THIS TRICYCLE HAVE?

HOW MANY
BALLOONS ARE RED?

HOW MANY BOYS ARE IN THE PICTURE?

JOHN ATE ONE APPLE
HOW MANY
ARE LEFT?

HOW MANY FISH ARE IN THIS BOWL?

HOW MANY
BOOKS ARE LEFT
ON THE SHELF?

HOW MANY LETTERS ARE ON THE DOORMAT?

HOW MANY SUNFLOWERS CAN YOU SEE?

HOW MANY CANDLES WILL BE ON YOUR CAKE NEXT YEAR?